2B

Contents

Use of guidance

THE APPROVED DOCUMENTS

This document is one of a series that has been approved and issued by the Secretary of State for the purpose of providing practical guidance with respect to the technical requirements of the Building Regulations 2000 for England and Wales.

At the back of this document is a list of all the documents that have been approved and issued by the Secretary of State for this purpose.

Approved Documents are intended to provide guidance for some of the more common building situations. However, there may well be alternative ways of achieving compliance with the requirements. Thus there is no obligation to adopt any particular solution contained in an Approved Document if you prefer to meet the relevant requirement in some other way.

OTHER REQUIREMENTS

The guidance contained in an Approved Document relates only to the particular requirements of the Regulations that the document addresses. The building work will also have to comply with the requirements of any other relevant paragraphs in Schedule 1 to the Regulations.

There are Approved Documents that give guidance on each of the Parts of Schedule 1 and on Regulation 7.

LIMITATION ON REQUIREMENTS

In accordance with Regulation 8, the requirements in Parts A to D, F to K and N (except for paragraphs H2 and J6) of Schedule 1 to the Building Regulations) do not require anything to be done except for the purpose of securing reasonable standards of health and safety for persons in or about buildings (and any others who may be affected by buildings or matters connected with buildings). This is one of the categories of purpose for which Building Regulations may be made.

Paragraphs H2 and J6 are excluded from Regulation 8 because they deal directly with prevention of the contamination of water. Parts E and M (which deal, respectively, with resistance to the passage of sound, and access to and use of buildings) are excluded from Regulation 8 because they address the welfare and convenience of building users. Part L is excluded from Regulation 8 because it addresses the conservation of fuel and power. All these matters are amongst the purposes, other than health and safety that may be addressed by Building Regulations.

MATERIALS AND WORKMANSHIP

Any building work which is subject to the requirements imposed by Schedule 1 to the Building Regulations should, in accordance with Regulation 7, be carried out with proper materials and in a workmanlike manner.

You may show that you have complied with Regulation 7 in a number of ways. These include the appropriate use of a product bearing CE marking in accordance with the Construction Products Directive (89/106/EEC)[1], the Low Voltage Directive (73/23/EEC and amendment 93/68 EEC)[2] and the EMC Directive (89/336/EEC)[3] as amended by the CE Marking Directive (93/68/EEC)[4] or a product complying with an appropriate technical specification (as defined in those Directives), a British Standard, or an alternative national technical specification of any state which is a contracting party to the European Economic Area which, in use, is equivalent, or a product covered by a national or European certificate issued by a European Technical Approval Issuing body, and the conditions of use are in accordance with the terms of the certificate. You will find further guidance in the Approved Document supporting Regulation 7 on materials and workmanship.

INDEPENDENT CERTIFICATION SCHEMES

There are many UK product certification schemes. Such schemes certify compliance with the requirements of a recognised document that is appropriate to the purpose for which the material is to be used. Materials which are not so certified may still conform to a relevant standard.

Many certification bodies that approve such schemes are accredited by UKAS.

TECHNICAL SPECIFICATIONS

Building Regulations are made for specific purposes: health and safety, energy conservation and the welfare and convenience of disabled people. Standards and technical approvals are relevant guidance to the extent that they relate to these considerations. However, they may also address other aspects of performance such as serviceability, or aspects which although they relate to health and safety are not covered by the Regulations.

---

[1]   As implemented by the Construction Products Regulations 1991 (SI 1991/1620).

[2]   As implemented by the Electrical Equipment (Safety) Regulations 1994 (SI 1994/3260).

[3]   As implemented by the Electromagnetic Compatibility Regulations 1992 (SI 1992/2372).

[4]   As implemented by the Construction Products (Amendment) Regulations 1994 (SI 1994/3051) and the Electromagnetic Compatibility (Amendment) Regulations 1994 (SI 1994/3080).

When an Approved Document makes reference to a named standard, the relevant version of the standard is the one listed at the end of the publication. However, if this version has been revised or updated by the issuing standards body, the new version may be used as a source of guidance provided it continues to address the relevant requirements of the Regulations.

The appropriate use of a product that complies with a European Technical Approval as defined in the Construction Products Directive will meet the relevant requirements.

The Office intends to issue periodic amendments to its Approved Documents to reflect emerging harmonised European Standards. Where a national standard is to be replaced by a European harmonised standard, there will be a coexistence period during which either standard may be referred to. At the end of the coexistence period the national standard will be withdrawn

THE WORKPLACE (HEALTH, SAFETY AND WELFARE) REGULATIONS 1992

The Workplace (Health, Safety and Welfare) Regulations 1992 as amended by The Health and Safety (Miscellaneous Amendments) Regulations 2002 (SI 2002/2174) contain some requirements which affect building design. The main requirements are now covered by the Building Regulations, but for further information see: *Workplace health, safety and welfare: Workplace (Health, Safety and Welfare) Regulations 1992, Approved Code of Practice, L24, HMSO, 1992* (ISBN 0 71760 413 6).

The Workplace (Health, Safety and Welfare) Regulations 1992 apply to the common parts of flats and similar buildings if people such as cleaners and caretakers are employed to work in these common parts. Where the requirements of the Building Regulations that are covered by this Part do not apply to dwellings, the provisions may still be required in the situations described above in order to satisfy the Workplace Regulations.

MIXED USE DEVELOPMENT

In mixed use developments part of a building may be used as a dwelling while another part has a non-domestic use. In such cases, if the requirements of this Part of the Regulations for dwellings and non-domestic use differ, the requirements for non-domestic use should apply in any shared parts of the building.

The Requirement

This Approved Document, which takes effect on 6 April 2006, deals with the energy efficiency requirements in the Building Regulations 2000 (as amended by SI 2001/3335 and SI 2006/652). The energy efficiency requirements are conveyed in Part L of Schedule 1 to the Regulations and regulations 4A, 17C and 17D as described below.

Requirement	*Limits on application*

Part L Conservation of fuel and power
 	
L1. Reasonable provision shall be made for the conservation of fuel and power in buildings by:
 	
    a. limiting heat gains and losses:
 	
        i. through thermal elements and other parts of the building fabric; and
 	
        ii. from pipes, ducts and vessels used for space heating, space cooling and hot water services;
 	
    b. providing and commissioning energy efficient fixed building services with effective controls; and
 	
    c. providing to the owner sufficient information about the building, the fixed building services and their maintenance requirements so that the building can be operated in such a manner as to use no more fuel and power than is reasonable in the circumstances.	

Other changes to the Regulations

There are new Regulations that introduce new energy efficiency requirements and other relevant changes to the existing regulations. For ease of reference the principal elements of the regulations that bear on energy efficiency are repeated below and, where relevant, in the body of the guidance in the rest of this Approved Document. However it must be recognised that the Statutory Instrument takes precedence if there is any doubt over interpretation.

Interpretation

Regulation 2(1) is amended to include the following new definitions.

'Change to a building's energy status' means any change which results in a building becoming a building to which the energy efficiency requirements of these Regulations apply, where previously it was not.

'Energy efficiency requirements' means the requirements of regulations 4A, 17C and 17D and Part L of Schedule 1.

'Fixed building services' means any part of, or any controls associated with:

a. fixed internal or external lighting systems, but does not include emergency escape lighting or specialist process lighting; or

b. fixed systems for heating, hot water service, air conditioning or mechanical ventilation.

'Renovation' in relation to a thermal element means the provision of a new layer in the thermal element or the replacement of an existing layer, but excludes decorative finishes, and 'renovate' shall be construed accordingly.

New paragraphs (2A) and (2B) are added to Regulation 2 as follows.

(2A) In these 'Thermal element' means a wall, floor or roof (but does not include windows, doors, roof windows or roof-lights) which separates a thermally conditioned part of the building ('the conditioned space') from:

a. the external environment (including the ground); or

b. in the case of floors and walls, another part of the building which is:

    i. unconditioned;

    ii an extension falling within class VII in Schedule 2; or

    iii. where this paragraph applies, conditioned to a different temperature,

    and includes all parts of the element between the surface bounding the conditioned space and the external environment or other part of the building as the case may be.

(2B) Paragraph (2A)(b)(iii) only applies to a building which is not a dwelling, where the other part of the building is used for a purpose which is not similar or identical to the purpose for which the conditioned space is used.

Meaning of building work

Regulation 3 is amended as follows.

3.–(1) In these Regulations 'building work' means:

a. the erection or extension of a building;

b. the provision or extension of a controlled service or fitting in or in connection with a building;

c. the material alteration of a building, or a controlled service or fitting, as mentioned in paragraph (2);

d. work required by regulation 6 (requirements relating to material change of use);

e. the insertion of insulating material into the cavity wall of a building;

f. work involving the underpinning of a building;

g. work required by regulation 4A (requirements relating to thermal elements);

h. work required by regulation 4B (requirements relating to a change of energy status);

i. work required by regulation 17D (consequential improvements to energy performance).

(2) An alteration is material for the purposes of these Regulations if the work, or any part of it, would at any stage result:

a. in a building or controlled service or fitting not complying with a relevant requirement where previously it did; or

b. in a building or controlled service or fitting which before the work commenced did not comply with a relevant requirement, being more unsatisfactory in relation to such a requirement.

(3) In paragraph (2) 'relevant requirement' means any of the following applicable requirements of Schedule 1, namely:

Part A (structure)
paragraph B1 (means of warning and escape)
paragraph B3 (internal fire spread – structure)
paragraph B4 (external fire spread)
paragraph B5 (access and facilities for the fire service)
Part M (access to and use of buildings).

Requirements relating to building work

Regulation 4 is amended as follows:

4.–(1) Subject to paragraph 1A building work shall be carried out so that:

   a.   it complies with the applicable requirements contained in Schedule 1; and

   b.   in complying with any such requirement there is no failure to comply with any other such requirement.

(1A) Where:

   a.   building work is of a kind described in regulation 3(1)(g), (h) or (i); and

   b.   the carrying out of that work does not constitute a material alteration,

   that work need only comply with the applicable requirements of Part L of Schedule 1.

(2) Building work shall be carried out so that, after it has been completed:

   a.   any building which is extended or to which a material alteration is made; or

   b.   any building in, or in connection with, which a controlled service or fitting is provided, extended or materially altered; or

   c.   any controlled service or fitting,

   complies with the applicable requirements of Schedule 1 or, where it did not comply with any such requirement, is no more unsatisfactory in relation to that requirement than before the work was carried out.

Requirements relating to thermal elements

A new regulation 4A is added as follows:

4A.–(1) Where a person intends to renovate a thermal element, such work shall be carried out as is necessary to ensure that the whole thermal element complies with the requirements of paragraph L1(a)(i) of Schedule 1.

(2) Where a thermal element is replaced, the new thermal element shall comply with the requirements of paragraph L1(a)(i) of Schedule 1.

Requirements relating to a change to energy status

A new regulation 4B is added as follows:

4B.–(1) Where there is a change to a building's energy status, such work, if any, shall be carried out as is necessary to ensure that the building complies with the applicable requirements of Part L of Schedule 1.

(2) In this regulation 'building' means the building as a whole or parts of it that have been designed or altered to be used separately.

Requirements relating to a material change of use

Regulation 6 is updated to take account of the changes to Part L.

Exempt buildings and work

Regulation 9 is substantially altered as follows.

9.–(1) Subject to paragraphs (2) and (3) these Regulations do not apply to:

   a.   the erection of any building or extension of a kind described in Schedule 2; or

   b.   the carrying out of any work to or in connection with such a building or extension, if after the carrying out of that work it is still a building or extension of a kind described in that Schedule.

(2) The requirements of Part P of Schedule 1 apply to:

   a.   any greenhouse;

   b.   any small detached building falling within class VI in Schedule 2; and

   c.   any extension of a building falling within class VII in Schedule 2,

which in any case receives its electricity from a source shared with or located inside a dwelling.

(3) The energy efficiency requirements of these Regulations apply to:

   a.   the erection of any building of a kind falling within this paragraph;

   b.   the extension of any such building, other than an extension falling within class VII in Schedule 2; and

   c.   the carrying out of any work to or in connection with any such building or extension.

(4) A building falls within paragraph (3) if it:

   a.   is a roofed construction having walls;

   b.   uses energy to condition the indoor climate; and

   c.   does not fall within the categories listed in paragraph (5).

(5) The categories referred to in paragraph (4)(c) are:

   a.   buildings which are:

      i.   listed in accordance with section 1 of the Planning (Listed Buildings and Conservation Areas) Act 1990;

      ii.   in a conservation area designated in accordance with section 69 of that Act; or

      iii. included in the schedule of monuments maintained under section 1 of the Ancient Monuments and Archaeological Areas Act 1979,

where compliance with the energy efficiency requirements would unacceptably alter their character or appearance;

b. buildings which are used primarily or solely as places of worship;

c. temporary buildings with a planned time of use of two years or less, industrial sites, workshops and non-residential agricultural buildings with low energy demand;

d. stand-alone buildings other than dwellings with a total useful floor area of less than 50m^2.

(6) In this regulation:

a. 'building' means the building as a whole or parts of it that have been designed or altered to be used separately; and

b. the following terms have the same meaning as in European Parliament and Council Directive 2002/91/EC on the energy performance of buildings:

  i.   'industrial sites';

  ii. 'low energy demand';

  iii. 'non-residential agricultural buildings';

  iv. 'places of worship';

  v.   'stand-alone';

  vi. 'total useful floor area';

  vii. 'workshops'.

Giving of a building notice or deposit of plans

Regulation 12 is substantially amended as follows.

12.–(1) In this regulation 'relevant use' means a use as a workplace of a kind to which Part II of the Fire Precautions (Workplace) Regulations 1997 applies or a use designated under section 1 of the Fire Precautions Act 1971.

(2) This regulation applies to a person who intends to:

a. carry out building work;

b. replace or renovate a thermal element in a building to which the energy efficiency requirements apply;

c. make a change to a building's energy status; or

d. make a material change of use.

(2A) Subject to the following provisions of this regulation, a person to whom this regulation applies shall:

a. give to the local authority a building notice in accordance with regulation 13; or

b. deposit full plans with the local authority in accordance with regulation 14.

(3) A person shall deposit full plans where he intends to carry out building work in relation to a building to which the Regulatory Reform (Fire Safety) Order 2005 applies, or will apply after the completion of the building work.

(4) A person shall deposit full plans where he intends to carry out work which includes the erection of a building fronting on to a private street.

(4A) A person shall deposit full plans where he intends to carry out building work in relation to which paragraph H4 of Schedule 1 imposes a requirement.

(5) A person who intends to carry out building work is not required to give a building notice or deposit full plans where the work consists only of work:

a. described in column 1 of the Table in Schedule 2A if the work is to be carried out by a person described in the corresponding entry in column 2 of that Table, and paragraphs 1 and 2 of that schedule have effect for the purposes of the descriptions in the Table; or

b. described in Schedule 2B.

(6) Where regulation 20 of the Building (Approved Inspectors etc.) Regulations 2000 (local authority powers in relation to partly completed work) applies, the owner shall comply with the requirements of that regulation instead of with this regulation.

(7) Where:

a. a person proposes to carry out work which consists of emergency repairs to any fixed building services in respect of which Part L of Schedule 1 imposes a requirement;

b. it is not practicable to comply with paragraph (2A) before commencing the work; and

c. paragraph (5) does not apply,

he shall give a building notice to the local authority as soon as reasonably practicable after commencement of the work.

Regulation 13 (particulars and plans where a building notice is given) and 14 (full plans)

These are amended to apply to renovation or replacement of a thermal element and a change to a building's energy status.

Provisions applicable to self-certification schemes

16A.–(1) This regulation applies to the extent that the building work consists only of work of a type described in column 1 of the Table in Schedule 2A and the work is carried out by a person who is described in the corresponding entry in column 2 of that Table in respect of that type of work.

(2) Where this regulation applies, the local authority is authorised to accept, as evidence that the requirements of regulations 4 and 7 have been satisfied, a certificate to that effect by the person carrying out the building work.

(3) Where this regulation applies, the person carrying out the work shall, not more than 30 days after the completion of the work:

a. give to the occupier a copy of the certificate referred to in paragraph (2); and

b. give to the local authority:

    i. notice to that effect, or

    ii. the certificate referred to in paragraph (2).

(4) Paragraph (3) of this regulation does not apply where a person carries out the building work described in Schedule 2B.

New Part VA

Energy Performance of buildings

New Regulations are added as follows.

Methodology of calculation of the energy performance of buildings

17A. The Secretary of State shall approve a methodology of calculation of the energy performance of buildings.

Minimum energy performance requirements for buildings

17B. The Secretary of State shall approve minimum energy performance requirements for new buildings, in the form of target CO_2 emission rates, which shall be based upon the methodology approved pursuant to regulation 17A.

New buildings

17C. Where a building is erected, it shall not exceed the target CO_2 emission rate for the building that has been approved pursuant to regulation 17B.

Consequential improvements to energy performance

17D.–(1) Paragraph (2) applies to an existing building with a total useful floor area over 1000m² where the proposed building work consists of or includes:

a. an extension;

b. the initial provision of any fixed building services; or

c. an increase to the installed capacity of any fixed building services.

(2) Subject to paragraph (3), where this regulation applies, such work, if any, shall be carried out as is necessary to ensure that the building complies with the requirements of Part L of Schedule 1.

(3) Nothing in paragraph (2) requires work to be carried out if it is not technically, functionally and economically feasible.

Interpretation

17E. In this Part 'building' means the building as a whole or parts of it that have been designed or altered to be used separately.

Part VI – Miscellaneous

New Regulations are added as follows.

Pressure testing

20B.–(1) This regulation applies to the erection of a building in relation to which paragraph L1(a)(i) of Schedule 1 imposes a requirement.

(2) Where this regulation applies, the person carrying out the work shall, for the purpose of ensuring compliance with regulation 17C and paragraph L1(a)(i) of Schedule 1:

a. ensure that:

   i. pressure testing is carried out in such circumstances as are approved by the Secretary of State; and

   ii. the testing is carried out in accordance with a procedure approved by the Secretary of State; and

b. subject to paragraph (5), give notice of the results of the testing to the local authority.

(3) The notice referred to in paragraph (2)(b) shall:

a. record the results and the data upon which they are based in a manner approved by the Secretary of State; and

b. be given to the local authority not later than seven days after the final test is carried out.

(4) A local authority is authorised to accept, as evidence that the requirements of paragraph (2)(a)(ii) have been satisfied, a certificate to that effect by a person who is registered by the British Institute of Non-destructive Testing in respect of pressure testing for the air tightness of buildings.

(5) Where such a certificate contains the information required by paragraph (3)(a), paragraph (2)(b) does not apply.

Commissioning

20C.–(1) This regulation applies to building work in relation to which paragraph L1(b) of Schedule 1 imposes a requirement, but does not apply where the work consists only of work described in Schedule 2B.

(2) Where this regulation applies the person carrying out the work shall, for the purpose of ensuring compliance with paragraph L1(b) of Schedule 1, give to the local authority a notice confirming that the fixed building services have been commissioned in accordance with a procedure approved by the Secretary of State.

(3) The notice shall be given to the local authority:

a. not later than the date on which the notice required by regulation 15(4) is required to be given; or

b. where that regulation does not apply, not more than 30 days after completion of the work.

CO_2 emission rate calculations

20D.–(1) Subject to paragraph (4), where regulation 17C applies the person carrying out the work shall provide to the local authority a notice which specifies:

a. the target CO_2 emission rate for the building; and

b. the calculated CO_2 emission rate for the building as constructed.

(2) The notice shall be given to the local authority not later than the date on which the notice required by regulation 20B is required to be given.

(3) A local authority is authorised to accept, as evidence that the requirements of regulation 17C would be satisfied if the building were constructed in accordance with an accompanying list of specifications, a certificate to that effect by a person who is registered by:

a. FAERO Limited; or

b. BRE Certification Limited,

in respect of the calculation of CO_2 emission rates of buildings.

(4) Where such a certificate is given to the local authority:

a. paragraph (1) does not apply; and

b. the person carrying out the work shall provide to the local authority not later than the date on which the notice required by regulation 20B is required to be given a notice which:

   i. states whether the building has been constructed in accordance with the list of specifications which accompanied the certificate; and

   ii. if it has not, lists any changes to the specifications to which the building has been constructed.

Schedule 2A

Schedule 2A is amended as follows:

Self-certification schemes and exemptions from requirement to give building notice or deposit full plans.

Column 1	Column 2
Type of work	*Person carrying out work*
1. Installation of a heat-producing gas appliance.	A person, or an employee of a person, who is a member of a class of persons approved in accordance with regulation 3 of the Gas Safety (Installation and Use) Regulations 1998.
2. Installation of heating or hot water service system connected to a heat-producing gas appliance, or associated controls.	A person registered by CORGI Services Limited in respect of that type of work.
3. Installation of: a. an oil-fired combustion appliance which has a rated heat output of 100 kilowatts or less and which is installed in a building with no more than 3 storeys (excluding any basement) or in a dwelling; b. oil storage tanks and the pipes connecting them to combustion appliances; or c. heating and hot water service systems connected to an oil-fired combustion appliance.	An individual registered by Oil Firing Technical Association Limited, NAPIT Certification Limited or Building Engineering Services Competence Accreditation Limited in respect of that type of work.
4. Installation of: a. a solid fuel burning combustion appliance which has a rated heat output of 50 kilowatts or less which is installed in a building with no more than 3 storeys (excluding any basement); or b. heating and hot water service systems connected to a solid fuel burning combustion appliance.	A person registered by HETAS Limited, NAPIT Certification Limited or Building Engineering Services Competence Accreditation Limited in respect of that type of work.
5. Installation of a heating or hot water service system, or associated controls, in a dwelling.	A person registered by Building Engineering Services Competence Accreditation Limited in respect of that type of work.
6. Installation of a heating, hot water service, mechanical ventilation or air conditioning system, or associated controls, in a building other than a dwelling.	A person registered by Building Engineering Services Competence Accreditation Limited in respect of that type of work.
7. Installation of an air conditioning or ventilation system in an existing dwelling, which does not involve work on systems shared with other dwellings.	A person registered by CORGI Services Limited or NAPIT Certification Limited in respect of that type of work.
8. Installation of a commercial kitchen ventilation system which does not involve work on systems shared with parts of the building occupied separately.	A person registered by CORGI Services Limited in respect of that type of work.
9. Installation of a lighting system or electric heating system, or associated electrical controls.	A person registered by The Electrical Contractors Association Limited in respect of that type of work.
10. Installation of fixed low or extra-low voltage electrical installations.	A person registered by BRE Certification Limited, British Standards Institution, ELECSA Limited, NICEIC Group Limited or NAPIT Certification Limited in respect of that type of work.
11. Installation of fixed low or extra-low voltage electrical installations as a necessary adjunct to or arising out of other work being carried out by the registered person.	A person registered by CORGI Services Limited, ELECSA Limited, NAPIT Certification Limited, NICEIC Group Limited or Oil Firing Technical Association Limited in respect of that type of electrical work.
12. Installation, as a replacement, of a window, rooflight, roof window or door (being a door which together with its frame has more than 50 per cent of its internal face area glazed) in an existing building.	A person registered under the Fenestration Self-Assessment Scheme by Fensa Ltd, or by CERTASS Limited or the British Standards Institution in respect of that type of work.

13. Installation of a sanitary convenience, washing facility or bathroom in a dwelling, which does not involve work on shared or underground drainage.	A person registered by CORGI Services Limited or NAPIT Certification Limited in respect of that type of work.

14.–(1) Subject to paragraph (2), any building work, other than the provision of a masonry chimney, which is necessary to ensure that any appliance, service or fitting which is installed and which is described in the preceding entries in column 1 above, complies with the applicable requirements contained in Schedule 1.
 	
(2) Paragraph (1) does not apply to:
 	
  c. building work which is necessary to ensure that a heat-producing gas appliance complies with the applicable requirements contained in Schedule 1 unless the appliance:
 	
     i. has a rated heat output of 100 kilowatts or less; and
 	
     ii. is installed in a building with no more than 3 storeys (excluding any basement), or in a dwelling; or
 	
  d. the provision of a masonry chimney.
	The person who installs the appliance, service or fitting to which the building work relates and who is described in the corresponding entry in column 2 above.

Schedule 2B

L2B Schedule 2B is amended as follows:

Descriptions of work where no building notice or deposit of full plans required.

1 Work consisting of:

a. replacing any fixed electrical equipment which does not include the provision of

   i. any new fixed cabling;

   ii. a new consumer unit; and

b. replacing a damaged cable for a single circuit only;

c. re-fixing or replacing enclosures of existing installation components, where the circuit protective measures are unaffected;

d. providing mechanical protection to an existing fixed installation, where the circuit protective measures and current carrying capacity of conductors are unaffected by the increased thermal insulation;

e. installing or upgrading main or supplementary equipotential bonding;

f. in heating or cooling systems:

   i. replacing control devices that utilise existing fixed control wiring or pneumatic pipes;

   ii. replacing a distribution system output device;

   iii. providing a valve or a pump;

   iv. providing a damper or fan;

g. in hot water service systems, providing a valve or pump;

h. replacing an external door (where the door together with its frame has not more than 50% of its internal face area glazed);

i. in existing buildings other than dwellings, providing fixed internal lighting where no more than 100m^2 of the floor area of the building is to be served by the lighting.

2 Work which:

a. is not in a kitchen, or a special location,

b. does not involve work on a special installation, and

c. consists of:

   i. adding light fittings and switches to an existing circuit; or

   ii. adding socket outlets and fused spurs to an existing ring or radial circuit;

3 Work on:

a. telephone wiring or extra-low voltage wiring for the purposes of communications, information technology, signalling, control and similar purposes, where the wiring is not in a special location;

b. equipment associated with the wiring referred to in sub-paragraph (a);

c. pre-fabricated equipment sets and associated flexible leads with integral plug and socket connections.

4 For the purposes of this Schedule:

'kitchen' means a room or part of a room which contains a sink and food preparation facilities;

'special installation' means an electric floor or ceiling heating system, an outdoor lighting or electric power installation, an electricity generator, or an extra-low voltage lighting system which is not a pre-assembled lighting set bearing the CE marking referred to in regulation 9 of the Electrical Equipment (Safety) Regulations 1994; and

'special location' means a location within the limits of the relevant zones specified for a bath, a shower, a swimming or paddling pool or a hot air sauna in the Wiring Regulations, sixteenth edition, published by the Institution of Electrical Engineers and the British Standards Institution as BS 7671: 2001 and incorporating amendments 1 and 2.

Section 0: General guidance

CONVENTIONS USED IN THIS DOCUMENT

1 In this document the following conventions have been adopted to assist understanding and interpretation:

a. Texts shown against a green background are extracts from the Building Regulations as amended and convey the legal requirements that bear on compliance with Part L. It should be remembered however that building works must comply with all the other relevant provisions. Similar provisions are conveyed by the Building (Approved Inspectors) Regulations as amended.

b. Key terms are printed in **bold italic text** and defined for the purposes of this Approved Document in Section 5 of this document.

c. References given as footnotes and repeated as endnotes are given as ways of meeting the requirements or as sources of more general information as indicated in the particular case. The Approved Document will be amended from time to time to include new references and to refer to revised editions where this aids compliance.

d. Additional *commentary in italic text* appears after some numbered paragraphs. The commentary is intended to assist understanding of the immediately preceding paragraph or sub-paragraph, but is not part of the approved guidance.

Types of work covered by this Approved Document

2 This Approved Document gives guidance on what, in ordinary circumstances, will meet the requirements of Regulation 4A, Regulation 17D and Part L when carrying out work on existing buildings that are not dwellings.

It should be noted that dwellings refer to self-contained units. **Rooms for residential purposes** *are not dwellings, and so Approved Document L2B applies to them.*

3 In particular, this Approved Document gives guidance relating to the following activities:

a. Consequential improvements (see paragraphs 14 to 23)

b. An extension (see paragraphs 24 to 33)

c. A material change of use (see paragraphs 34 to 37)

d. A material alteration (see paragraphs 38 to 39).

e. The provision or extension of a controlled service or fitting (see paragraphs 40 to 78)

f. The replacement or **renovation** of a **thermal element** (see paragraphs 79 to 88)

4 In certain types of work in relation to an existing building, it may be more appropriate to utilise the guidance from the other Part L Approved Documents. The following sub-paragraphs identify some of the circumstances in which this might be appropriate.

a. **Fit-out works**:

  i. in buildings erected in compliance with the Building Regulations in force before 6 April 2006 must comply with the **energy efficiency requirements** that came into effect on that date and ways of doing so are given in this Approved Document.

  ii. in buildings such as shell and core office buildings or business park units built in compliance with the energy efficiency requirements that came into effect on 6 April 2006 may need to be approached differently. Reasonable provision in these cases would be to comply with the **energy efficiency requirements** and to provide **fixed building services** that have efficiencies no worse than those assumed in the calculations showing the existing building complied with Regulation 17C when originally completed. In these cases it would be reasonable to make no further improvement to comply with Regulation 17D.

b. Large extensions (as defined in paragraph 25 of this Approved Document) should be carried out in accordance with the guidance in Approved Document L2A. However, Regulation 17D (consequential improvements) would apply and the guidance set out in this Approved Document would be relevant.

c. Where the work involves constructing an extension to an existing building using sub-assemblies that have been obtained from a centrally held stock or from the disassembly or relocation of buildings at other premises, the guidance in Approved Document L2A should be followed but Regulation 17D (consequential works) would also apply.

An example would be where a school is extended using prefabricated portable buildings.

d. Where the work involves a building that either before the work or after the work is completed contains one or more dwellings, the guidance in Approved Document L1B would apply to each **dwelling**.

It should be noted that dwellings refer to self-contained units. **Rooms for residential purposes** *are not dwellings, and so this Approved Document applies to them.*

5 The **energy efficiency requirements**, apart from those in Regulation 17C, apply to work in existing buildings. In most instances, this will require the **BCB** to be notified of the intended work before the work commences, either in the form of a deposit of full plans or by a building notice. In certain situations however other procedures apply. These include:

a. Where the work is being carried out under the terms of an approved Competent Persons self-certification (CP) scheme. In these cases, in accordance with Regulation 16A and Schedule 2A[5] no advance notification to the **BCB** is needed. At the completion of the work, the approved Competent Person provides the building owner with a certificate confirming that the installation has been carried out in accordance with the relevant requirements, and the scheme operator notifies the local authority to that effect.

b. Where the work involves an emergency repair, e.g. a failed boiler or a leaking hot water cylinder. In these cases, in accordance with Regulation 12(7)[6], there is no need to delay making the repair in order to make an advance notification to the building control body. However, in such cases it will still be necessary for the work to comply with the requirements and to give a notice to the **BCB** at the earliest opportunity, unless an installer registered under an appropriate CP scheme carries out the work. A completion certificate can then be issued in the normal way.

c. Where the work is of a minor nature as described in Schedule 2B[7] of the Building Regulations. Again, the work must comply with the relevant requirements, but need not be notified to the **BCB**.

TECHNICAL RISK

6 Building work must satisfy all the technical requirements set out in Regulations 4A, 17D and Schedule 1 of the Building Regulations. Part B (Fire safety), Part E (Resistance to the passage of sound), Part F (Ventilation), Part C (Site preparation and resistance to moisture), Part J (Combustion appliances and fuel storage systems) and Part P (Electrical safety in dwellings) are particularly relevant when considering the incorporation of energy efficiency measures.

7 The inclusion of any particular energy efficiency measure should not involve excessive technical risk. BR 262[8] provides general guidance on avoiding risks in the application of thermal insulation.

HISTORIC BUILDINGS

8 Special considerations apply if the building on which the work is to be carried out has special historic or architectural value and compliance with the **energy efficiency requirements** would unacceptably alter the character or appearance[9].

9 When undertaking work on or in connection with buildings with special historic or architectural value, the aim should be to improve energy efficiency where and to the extent that it is practically possible. This is provided that the work does not

prejudice the character of the host building or increase the risk of long-term deterioration to the building fabric or fittings. The guidance given in the English Heritage publication[10] should be taken into account in determining appropriate energy performance standards for such building works. Particular issues relating to work in historic buildings that warrant sympathetic treatment and where advice from others could therefore be beneficial include:

a. restoring the historic character of a building that has been subject to previous inappropriate alteration, e.g. replacement windows, doors and rooflights;

b. rebuilding a former building (e.g. following a fire or filling a gap site in a terrace);

c. making provisions enabling the fabric of historic buildings to 'breathe' to control moisture and potential long term decay problems.

10 In arriving at a balance between historic building conservation and energy efficiency improvements, it would be appropriate to take into account the advice of the local authority's conservation officer.

CALCULATION OF U-VALUES

11 U-values shall be calculated using the methods and conventions set out in BR 443[11], 'Conventions for U-value calculations'. The CAB/CWCT publication[12] gives guidance on the thermal performance of curtain walling.

12 The U-values for roof windows and rooflights given in this Approved Document are based on the particular U-value having been assessed with the roof window or rooflight in the vertical position. If a particular unit has been assessed in a plane other than the vertical, the standards given in this Approved Document should be modified by making a U-value adjustment following the guidance given in BR 443.

The stated standard for a replacement plastic rooflight as given in Table 4 is 2.2W/m²·K. This is for the unit assessed in the vertical plane. If the performance of a triple skin rooflight was assessed in the horizontal plane, then based on the guidance given in BR 443, the standard would be adjusted by 0.3W/m²·K (the value from BR 443 for a horizontal triple skin rooflight), requiring the rooflight as assessed in the horizontal plane to achieve a standard of 2.2 + 0.3 = 2.5W/m²·K.

---

5   Copies of these can be seen on pages 9 and 12.

6   A copy of this can be seen on page 8.

7   A copy of this can be seen on page 14.

8   BR 262 *Thermal insulation: avoiding risks*, BRE, 2001.

9   See the copy of regulation 9 on page 7.

10   *Building Regulations and Historic Buildings*, English Heritage, 2002 (revised 2004).

11   BR 443 *Conventions for U-value calculations*, BRE, 2006.

12   *The thermal assessment of window assemblies, curtain walling and non-traditional building envelopes*, CWCT, 2006, ISBN 1 87400 338 6.

BUILDINGS THAT ARE EXEMPT FROM THE REQUIREMENTS IN PART L

13 The provisions for exempting buildings and building work from the Building Regulations requirements have changed and the new provisions are given in regulation 9.

17

Section 1: Consequential improvements

14 Regulation 17D states:

> **17D.**–(1) Paragraph (2) applies to an existing building with a total useful floor area over 1000m² where the proposed building work consists of or includes:
>
> a. an extension;
>
> b. the initial provision of any fixed building services; or
>
> c. an increase to the installed capacity of any fixed building services.
>
> (2) Subject to paragraph (3), where this regulation applies, such work, if any, shall be carried out as is necessary to ensure that the building complies with the requirements of Part L of Schedule 1.
>
> (3) Nothing in paragraph (2) requires work to be carried out if it is not technically, functionally and economically feasible.

15 Regulation 17E defines 'building' in regulation 17D as follows:

> **17E** In this Part 'building' means the building as a whole or parts of it that have been designed or altered to be used separately.

These regulations implement Article 6 of the Energy Performance of Buildings Directive.

16 Where regulation 17D applies, **consequential improvements**, in addition to the proposed building work (the **principal works**), should be made to ensure that the building complies with Part L, to the extent that such improvements are technically, functionally and economically feasible. Paragraphs 17 to 23 below set out guidance on what will constitute technically, functionally and economically feasible consequential improvements in various circumstances.

The principal works must comply with the energy efficiency requirements in the normal way.

17 Measures that achieve a **simple payback** not exceeding 15 years will be economically feasible unless there are unusual circumstances.

For example, if the remaining life of the building is less than 15 years it would only be economic to carry out improvements with payback periods within that life.

Regulation 17D(1)(a) – Consequential improvements on extending a building

Constructing a new free-standing building on an existing site (e.g. a new out-patients building at an existing hospital site, or a new classroom block at a school) is not an extension. These should be treated as new buildings.

18 Where a building is extended, a way of complying with the Requirement 17D would be to adopt measures such as those in Table 1 to the extent that their value is not less than 10% of the value of the principal works. The value of the **principal works** and the value of the **Consequential improvements** should be established using prices current at the date the proposals are made known to the **BCB**. They should be made known by way of a report signed by a suitably qualified person as part of the initial notice or deposit of plans.

An example of a suitably qualified person would be a chartered quantity surveyor.

Table 1	**Improvements that in ordinary circumstances are practical and economically feasible**

Items 1 to 7 will usually meet the economic feasibility criterion set out in paragraph 17. A shorter payback period is given in item 8 because such measures are likely to be more capital intensive or more risky than the others.

1 Upgrading heating systems more than 15 years old by the provision of new plant or improved controls

2 Upgrading cooling systems more than 15 years old by the provision of new plant or improved controls

3 Upgrading air-handling systems more than 15 years old by the provision of new plant or improved controls

4 Upgrading general lighting systems that have an average lamp efficacy of less than 40 lamp-lumens per circuit-watt and that serve areas greater than 100m² by the provision of new luminaires or improved controls

5 Installing energy metering following the guidance given in CIBSE TM 39[13]

6 Upgrading **thermal elements** which have U-values worse than those set out in column (a) of Table 7 following the guidance in paragraphs 87 and 88

7 Replacing existing windows, roof windows or rooflights (but excluding **display windows**) or doors (but excluding **high usage entrance doors**) which have a U-value worse than 3.3W/m²·K following the guidance in paragraphs 75 to 78

8 Increasing the on-site low and zero carbon (LZC) energy-generating systems if the existing on-site systems provide less than 10% of on-site energy demand, provided the increase would achieve a **simple payback** of seven years or less. The ODPM publication[14] gives advice on appraising the feasibility of such systems

---

[13] TM 39 *Building Energy Metering*, CIBSE, 2006.

[14] *Low or Zero Carbon Energy Sources: Strategic Guide*, NBS, 2006.

Regulation 17D: Consequential improvements on installing building services

19 Where it is proposed to install a fixed building service as a first installation, or as an installation which increases the installed capacity per unit area of an existing service, reasonable provision would be to:

a. firstly improve those parts of the building served by the service, where this is economically feasible; and

This means for example that if heating systems are to be installed for the first time in a building or part thereof, or the installed heating capacity per unit area of an existing system is to be increased, the fabric should be improved. The aim in these cases is to make cost-effective improvements to the performance of the fabric so that the installed capacity (and the initial cost) of the fixed building services and their subsequent energy consumption are not excessive.

b. then, additionally, make improvements in line with the guidance in paragraph 16. The cost of any improvement made as a result of following the guidance set out in paragraph 19a) cannot be taken as contributing to the value of the consequential improvements specified in paragraph 16.

If only the improvements under a) were made, then the CO$_2$ emissions from the building might well increase as a result of the higher level of servicing. By also requiring the general improvements in b), an overall improvement should be achieved.

20 For the purposes of these Regulations, the installed capacity of a fixed building service is defined as the design output of the distribution system output devices (the terminal units) serving the space in question, divided by the **total useful floor area** of that space.

This means that if (e.g.) the size of central boiler plant is increased to serve a new extension rather than to increase the heating provision in the existing building, the consequential improvements required by paragraph 18 would be required but those required by the following paragraphs would not apply.

21 Reasonable provision for improving those parts of the building served by the service would be to follow the guidance in paragraphs 22 to 23 to the extent that the work is technically, functionally and economically feasible. The extent of such work is not limited by any 10% threshold. The following paragraphs give guidance on what in normal circumstances would be economically feasible.

22 Where the installed capacity per unit area of a heating system is increased:

a. The **thermal elements** within the area served which have U-values worse than those set out in column (a) of Table 7, should be upgraded following the guidance in paragraphs 87 and 88; and

b. Existing windows, roof windows or rooflights (but excluding **display windows**) or doors (but excluding **high usage entrance doors**) within the area served and which have U-values worse than 3.3W/m²·K should be replaced following the guidance in paragraphs 75 to 78.

23 Where the installed capacity per unit area of a cooling system is increased:

a. **Thermal elements** within heated areas which have U-values worse than those set out in column (a) of Table 7, should be upgraded following the guidance in paragraphs 87 and 88; and

b. If the area of windows, roof windows (but excluding **display windows**) within the area served exceeds 40% of the façade area or the area of rooflights exceeds 20% of the area of the roof and the design solar load exceeds 25W/m², then the solar control provisions should be upgraded such that at least one of the following three criteria is met:

 i. the design solar load is no greater than 25W/m²;

 ii. the design solar load is reduced by at least 20%;

 iii. the effective g-value is no worse than 0.3; and

This will reduce the solar gain and hence the space cooling demand. The calculation of effective g-value is explained in CIBSE TM 37[15].

c. Any lighting system within the area served by the relevant fixed building service which has an average lamp efficacy of less than 40 lamp-lumens per circuit watt, should be upgraded with new luminaires and/or controls following the guidance in paragraphs 54 to 63.

This will reduce lighting load and hence the space cooling demand.

---

[15] TM 37 *Design for improved solar shading control*, CIBSE, 2006.

Section 2: Guidance relating to building work

EXTENSIONS

24 The construction of an extension triggers the requirement for a consequential improvement in buildings with a **total useful floor area** greater than 1000m². In such cases, the guidance in Section 1 should be followed in addition to the following specific guidance.

Large extensions

25 Where the proposed extension has a total useful floor area that is both:

a. Greater than 100m²; and

b. Greater than 25% of the **total useful floor area** of the existing building

then the work should be regarded as a new building and the guidance in Approved Document L2A followed. The requirement for a consequential improvement should also be met by following the guidance in paragraph 16 of this Approved Document.

Other extensions

Fabric standards

26 Reasonable provision would be for the proposed extension to achieve the following performance standards:

a. Controlled fittings that meet the standards set out in paragraphs 75 to 78 of this Approved Document.

b. Newly constructed **thermal elements** that meet the standards set out in paragraphs 79 to 84 of this Approved Document.

c. Existing opaque fabric that becomes part of the thermal envelope of the building whereas previously it was not should meet the standards in paragraphs 87 and 88.

27 The area of windows and rooflights in the extension should not exceed the values given in Table 2, unless a greater proportion of glazing is present in the part of the building to which the extension is attached. In such cases, reasonable provision would be to limit the proportion of glazing in the extension so that it is no greater than the proportion that exists in the part of the building to which it is attached.

Table 2 Opening areas in the extension

Building type	Windows and personnel doors as % of exposed wall	Rooflights as % of area of roof
Residential buildings where people temporarily or permanently reside	30	20
Places of assembly, offices and shops	40	20
Industrial and storage buildings	15	20
Vehicle access doors and **display windows** and similar glazing	As required	N/A
Smoke vents	N/A	As required

Building services systems in the extension

28 Where ***fixed building services*** are provided or extended as part of constructing the extension, reasonable provision would be to follow the guidance in paragraphs 41 to 74.

Optional approaches with more design flexibility

29 The U-values given in paragraph 26 and the opening areas given in paragraph 27 may be varied provided that:

In industrial buildings, rooflights are a beneficial source of daylight, and so significant reductions in rooflight area could result in increased use of electric lighting. The NARM guidance[16] gives guidance on this issue.

a. the area weighted U-value of all the elements in the extension is no greater than that of an extension of the same size and shape that complies with the U-value standards referred to in paragraph 26 and the opening area in paragraph 27; and

The area-weighted U-value is given by the following expression:

$$\{(U_1 \times A_1) + (U_2 \times A_2) + (U_3 \times A_3) + ...)\}$$
$$\div \{(A_1 + A_2 + A_3 + ...)\}$$

b. the area weighted U-value for each element type is no worse than the value given in column (a) of Table 3; and

c. the U-value of any individual element is no worse than the relevant value in column (b) of Table 3.

To minimise condensation risk in localised parts of the envelope. An individual element is defined as those areas of the given element type that have same construction details. In the case of windows, doors and rooflights, the assessment should be based on the whole unit (i.e. in the case of a window, the combined performance of the glazing and frame).

30 Where even greater design flexibility is required, reasonable provision would be to use an approved calculation tool to demonstrate that the calculated CO_2 emissions from the building and proposed extension is no greater than for the building plus a notional extension complying with the standards of paragraphs 26 and 27. In these cases the area-weighted average U-value of each element type should be no worse than the standards set out in column (a) of Table 3, and the U-value of any individual element should be no worse than the values in column (b) of Table 3. For this calculation, the building used in the calculation of both the notional and actual extension should incorporate the improvements proposed to meet the requirement for a consequential improvement (see paragraph 16).

31 Where additional upgrades are proposed in the actual building to compensate for lower performance in the extension, then such upgrades should be implemented to a standard that is no worse than set out in the relevant guidance contained in this Approved Document. The relevant standards for upgrading retained thermal elements are as set out in column (b) of Table 7.

Where it is proposed to upgrade, then the standards set out in this Approved Document are cost effective and should be implemented in full. It will be worthwhile implementing them even if the improvement is more than necessary to achieve compliance. In some cases therefore, the standard of the extended building may be better than that required by paragraph 30 alone. Paragraph 31 ensures that no cost-effective improvement opportunities are traded away.

Table 3 **Limiting U-value standards (W/m²·K)**

Element	a. Area-weighted average U-value	b. Limiting U-value
Wall	0.35	0.70
Floor	0.25	0.70
Roof	0.25	0.35
Windows, roof windows, rooflights and doors[1]	2.2	3.3

Note:
1. See paragraph 14.

---

[16] *Use of rooflights to satisfy the 2002 Building Regulations for the Conservation of Fuel and Power*, NARM, 2003.

Conservatories

32 Where the extension is a **conservatory** that is not exempt by Regulation 9(3)[17], then reasonable provision would be to provide:

a. Effective thermal separation from the heated area in the existing **building**. The walls, doors and windows between the **building** and the extension should be insulated and draught-stripped to at least the same extent as in the existing **building**.

If a highly glazed extension is not thermally separated from the building, then it should be regarded as a conventional extension. Compliance in such cases could be demonstrated using the approach set out in paragraphs 26 to 31.

b. Independent temperature and on/off controls to any heating system. Any heating appliance should also conform to the standards set out in paragraph 41.

c. Glazed elements should comply with the standards given in column (b) of Table 5 and any opaque elements should have U-values that are no worse than the standards given in column (b) of Table 3.

Conservatories built at ground level and with a floor area no greater than 30m² are exempt from the Building Regulations (other than having to satisfy the requirements of Part N).

33 If a substantially glazed extension fails to qualify as a **conservatory** because it has less than the minimum qualifying amounts of translucent material, but otherwise satisfies paragraph 32, reasonable provision would be to demonstrate that the performance is no worse than a **conservatory** of the same size and shape. A way of doing so would be to show the area-weighted U-value of the elements in the proposed extension is no greater than that of a **conservatory** that complies with the standards set out in paragraph 32.

MATERIAL CHANGE OF USE AND CHANGE OF ENERGY STATUS

34 Material change of use is defined in Regulation 5 as follows:

For the purposes of paragraph 8(1)(e) of Schedule 1 to the Act and for the purposes of these Regulations, there is a material change of use where there is a change in the purposes for which or the circumstances in which a building is used, so that after that change:

a. the building is used as a dwelling, where previously it was not;

b. the building contains a flat, where previously it did not;

c. the building is used as an hotel or a boarding house, where previously it was not;

d. the building is used as an institution, where previously it was not;

e. the building is used as a public building, where previously it was not;

f. the building is not a building described in Classes I to VI in Schedule 2, where previously it was;

g. the building, which contains at least one dwelling, contains a greater or lesser number of dwellings than it did previously;

h. the building contains a room for residential purposes, where previously it did not;

i. the building, which contains at least one room for residential purposes, contains a greater or lesser number of such rooms than it did previously; or

j. the building is used as a shop where previously it was not.

35 When carrying out a material change of use, the Reasonable provision would be:

a. when carrying out a material change of use; or

b. when a building changes its energy status

to follow the guidance in paragraph 25.

36 In ordinary circumstances, reasonable provision would be:

a. Where controlled services or fittings are being provided or extended, to meet the standards set out in paragraphs 40 to 76 of this Approved Document.

b. Where the work involves the provision of a **thermal element**, to meet the standards set out in paragraphs 79 to 84 of this Approved Document.

For the purposes of Building Regulations provision means both new and replacement elements.

c. Where **thermal elements** are being renovated, to meet the guidance in paragraphs 85 and 86 of this Approved Document.

d. Any **thermal element** that is being retained should be upgraded following the guidance given in paragraphs 87 and 88 of this Approved Document.

e. Any existing window (including roof window or rooflight) or door which separates a conditioned space from an unconditioned space or the external environment and which has a U-value that is worse than 3.3W/m²·K, should be replaced following the guidance in paragraphs 75 to 78 unless they are **display windows** or **high usage entrance doors**. It would be reasonable in these latter cases to make some lesser provision for energy efficiency.

---

[17]   See the copy of Regulation 9 on page 7.

Option providing more design flexibility

37 To provide more design flexibility, an approved calculation tool can be used to demonstrate that the CO_2 emissions from the building as it will become are no worse than if the building had been improved following the guidance set out in paragraph 36. In these cases the U-values of any individual element should be no worse than the values in column (b) of Table 3.

MATERIAL ALTERATION

38 Material alterations are defined in Regulation 3(2) as follows.

3(2) An alteration is material for the purposes of these Regulations if the work, or any part of it, would at any stage result:

a. in a building or controlled service or fitting not complying with a relevant requirement where previously it did; or

b. in a building or controlled service or fitting which before the work commenced did not comply with a relevant requirement, being more unsatisfactory in relation to such a requirement.

3(3) In paragraph (2) 'relevant requirement' means any of the following applicable requirements of Schedule 1, namely:

a. Part A (structure)

b. Paragraph B1 (means of warning and escape)

c. Paragraph B3 (internal fire spread – structure)

d. Paragraph B4 (external fire spread)

e. Paragraph B5 (access and facilities for the fire service)

f. Part M (access to and use of buildings).

39 When carrying out a material alteration, reasonable provision would be:

a. when the work involves the provision of a **thermal element**, to follow the guidance in paragraphs 79 to 84 of this Approved Document.

For the purposes of Building Regulations, provision means both new and replacement elements.

b. when renovating a **thermal element**, to follow the guidance in paragraphs 85 and 86 of this Approved Document.

c. where an existing element becomes part of the thermal envelope of the building whereas previously it was not, to follow the guidance in paragraph 87 to 88. Any existing window (including roof window or rooflight) or door which becomes part of the thermal envelope where previously it was not and which has a U-value that is worse than 3.3W/m²·K, should be replaced following the guidance in paragraphs

75 to 78 unless they are **display windows** and **high usage entrance doors.** It would be reasonable in these latter cases to make some lesser provisions for energy efficiency.

d. when providing a controlled fitting, to follow the guidance on controlled fittings given in paragraphs 75 to 78 of this Approved Document.

e. when providing or extending a controlled service, to follow the guidance on controlled services given in paragraphs 40 to 74 of this Approved Document.

WORK ON CONTROLLED SERVICES AND FITTINGS

40 A controlled service or fitting is defined in Regulation 2(1) as follows:

'controlled service or fitting' means a service or fitting in relation to which Part G, H, J, L or P of Schedule 1 imposes a requirement;

Controlled services

41 Where the work involves the provision or extension of controlled services, reasonable provision would be to:

a. Provide new **fixed building services** that meet reasonable standards of energy efficiency, which in normal circumstances would be an efficiency not less than:

  i. The efficiencies set out in paragraphs 42 to 65; and

  ii. For central plant (i.e. boilers, chillers and main air handling plant), an efficiency that is not less than that of the controlled service being replaced. If the new service uses a different fuel, then the efficiency of the new appliance should be multiplied by the ratio of the CO_2 emission factor of the fuel used in the appliance being replaced to that of the fuel used in the new appliance before making this check (see Table 2 in Approved Document L2A for CO_2 emission factors).

This will prevent an existing low carbon component being replaced by a lesser provision. When fuel switching, if an existing chiller with a CoP of 2.5 is replaced by an absorption chiller with a CoP of 0.8 but fired by waste heat, the equivalent efficiency of the absorption chiller would be 0.8 x (0.422/0.018)=18.8, and so test (ii) would be satisfied. 0.422 and 0.018 kgCO₂/kWh are the emission factors for electricity and waste heat respectively as obtained from the table in ADL2A.

b. Provide new HVAC systems with appropriate controls to achieve reasonable standards of energy efficiency. In normal circumstances reasonable provision would be to provide the following control features on each system in addition to the system specific controls detailed in subsequent paragraphs.

i. The fixed building services systems should be sub-divided into separate control zones to correspond to each area of the building that has a significantly different solar exposure, occupancy period, or type of use.

ii. Each separate control zone should be capable of independent switching and control set-point.

iii. The provision of the service should respond to the requirements of the space it serves. If both heating and cooling are provided, they should be controlled so they do not operate simultaneously.

iv. Central plant serving the zone-based systems should only operate as and when required. The default condition should be off.

v. In addition to these general control requirements, the systems should meet specific control requirements and basic efficiency criteria as set out in the service-specific paragraphs beginning at paragraph 42.

c. Provide new lighting systems with appropriate controls to achieve reasonable standards of energy efficiency. In normal circumstances, reasonable provision would be to provide controls in accordance with the guidance in paragraphs 54 to 66; and

d. Demonstrate the new service has been effectively commissioned (see paragraphs 70 to 74); and

e. Demonstrate that reasonable provision of energy meters has been made for effective monitoring of the performance of newly installed plant (see paragraphs 67 to 69); and

f. Demonstrate that the relevant information has been recorded in a new log book or incorporated into an update of the existing one as described in paragraphs 89 to 92.

Heating and hot water systems

42 Reasonable provision for the performance of heating and hot water systems would be:

43 The use of heat-raising appliance(s) with an efficiency not less than that recommended for their type in the Non-domestic Heating, Cooling and Ventilation Compliance Guide (NDHCV Guide)[18], and

a. the provision of controls that meet the minimum control requirements as given in the NDHCV Guide for the particular type of appliance and heat distribution system.

44 The compliance checklists included in the NDHCV Guide are a useful tool in demonstrating that reasonable provision has been made.

Cooling plant

45 Where it is practical and cost effective to do so, measures to reduce cooling loads (e.g. through improved solar control or more efficient lighting) should be incorporated as part of any work to replace a chiller. BR 364[19] offers guidance on solar control strategies.

The cost of the improved solar control and/or lighting can be at least partially offset by the reduction in capital cost of the smaller chiller. Further savings will be made by reduced running costs.

46 Reasonable provision for the performance of cooling plant would be:

a. the use of equipment with an efficiency not less than that recommended for its type in the NDHCV Guide; and

b. the provision of controls that meet the minimum control requirements as given in the NDHCV Guide for the particular type of equipment and distribution system.

47 The compliance checklists included in the NDHCV Guide are a useful tool in demonstrating that reasonable provision has been made.

Air handling plant

48 Reasonable provision for the performance of air handling plant would be to follow the guidance in the Non-domestic Heating, Cooling and Ventilation Compliance Guide in providing:

a. suitably efficient air handling plant; and

b. energy-effective control systems.

49 In addition, the system should be capable of achieving a specific fan power at 25% of design flow rate which is no greater than that achieved at 100% design flow rate.

50 In order to aid commissioning and to provide flexibility for future changes of use, reasonable provision would be to equip with variable speed drives those fans that are rated at more than 1100W and which form part of the environmental control system(s). Smoke control fans and similar therefore fall outside this guidance.

51 In order to limit air leakage, ventilation ductwork should be constructed and assembled so as to be reasonably airtight. One way of achieving this is to comply with the specifications given in HVCA DW144[20].

---

[18]   *Non-domestic Heating, Cooling and Ventilation Compliance Guide*, NBS, 2006.

[19]   BR 364 *Solar Shading of Buildings*, BRE, 1999.

[20]   DW/144 *Specification for Sheet Metal Ductwork*, HVCA, 1998.

Insulation of pipes, ducts and vessels

52 Provision should be made for insulating hot and chilled water pipework and storage vessels, refrigerant pipework and ventilation ductwork to conserve energy and to maintain the temperature of the heating or cooling service.

53 Reasonable provision would be demonstrated by following the guidance in the Non-domestic heating, cooling and ventilation compliance guide.

The TIMSA Guide[21] explains the derivation of the performance standards and how they can be interpreted in practice.

Fixed internal lighting

54 Reasonable provision would be to install new systems that meet the criteria in paragraphs 55 to 66, depending on the use of the space.

When the area covered by the new lighting system is less than 100m², the work should still comply with the standards, but need not be notified to BCBs (see Schedule 2B).

GENERAL LIGHTING EFFICACY IN OFFICE, INDUSTRIAL AND STORAGE AREAS IN ALL BUILDING TYPES

55 For the purposes of this Approved Document, 'office' includes those areas that involve predominantly desk-based tasks, including classrooms, seminar rooms and conference rooms, including those in schools.

56 Reasonable provision would be to provide lighting with an average efficacy of not less than 45 luminaire-lumens/circuit-watt as averaged over the whole area of these space types in the building.

This allows design flexibility to vary the light output ratio of the luminaire and the luminous efficacy of the lamp.

57 The average luminaire-lumens/circuit-watt is calculated by:

(Lamp-lumens x LOR) summed for all luminaires in the relevant areas of the building, divided by the total (circuit watts x control factor) for all the luminaires where:

a. Lamp-lumens = the sum of the average initial (100 hour) lumen output of all the lamp(s) in the luminaire; and

b. LOR = the light output ratio of the luminaire, which means the ratio of the total light output of a luminaire under stated practical conditions to that of the lamp or lamps contained in the luminaire under reference conditions.

c. Control factor = the factor applicable when automatic controls substantially reduce the power consumption of the luminaire when electric light is not required (see commentary at paragraph 60, which includes values of the control factor for use in the above formula).

The controls factor is included in Approved Document L2B to allow greater flexibility and to encourage better controls.

GENERAL LIGHTING EFFICACY IN ALL OTHER TYPES OF SPACE

58 For lighting systems serving other than office or storage space, it may be appropriate to provide luminaires for which photometric data is not available or luminaires that are lower powered and use less efficient lamps. For such spaces, the requirements would be met if the installed lighting has an average initial (100 hour) lamp plus ballast efficacy of not less than 50 lamp-lumens per circuit-Watt.

LIGHTING CONTROLS FOR GENERAL LIGHTING IN ALL TYPES OF SPACE

59 Lighting controls should be provided so as to avoid unnecessary lighting during the times when daylight levels are adequate or when spaces are unoccupied. However, the operation of automatically switched lighting systems should be the subject of a risk assessment for safety and suitability.

60 Reasonable provision would be local switches in easily accessible positions within each working area or at boundaries between working areas and general circulation routes that are operated by the deliberate action of the occupants (referred to as occupant control), either manually or remotely.

Manual switches include rocker switches, push buttons and pull cords. Remote switches include wireless transmitters and telephone handset controls. For the purposes of Approved Document L, reference to switches includes dimmer switches and switching includes dimming. As a general rule, dimming should be effected by reducing rather than diverting the energy supply.

61 The distance on plan from any local switch to any luminaire it controls should generally be not more than six metres, or twice the height of the light fitting above the floor if this is greater. Where a space is a *daylit space* served by side windows, the perimeter row of lighting should in general be separately switched.

62 Occupant control of local switching can be supplemented by other controls such as automatic systems which:

a. switch the lighting off when they sense the absence of occupants; or

b. either dim or switch the lighting off when there is sufficient daylight.

Table 4 gives the control factors for such enhanced controls, which can be used as part of achieving the luminaire efficacy set out in paragraph 56.

When installed in appropriate locations, such enhanced control systems will deliver an energy benefit that can be traded against other aspects of the lighting system using the factors listed in Table 5.

---

[21] *HVAC Guidance for Achieving Compliance with Part L of the Building Regulations*, TIMSA 2006.

Table 4 **Luminaire control factors**

Control function	Control Factor
(a) The luminaire is in a daylit space and its light output is controlled by photoelectric switching or dimming control, with or without manual override.	0.90
(b) The luminaire is in a space that is likely to be unoccupied for a significant proportion of working hours and where a sensor switches off the lighting in the absence of occupants but switching on is done manually, except where this would be unsafe Central mechanical ventilation with heating and cooling	0.90
(c) Circumstances (a) and (b) combined	0.85
(d) None of the above	1.00

63 An alternative way of meeting the requirement would be to follow the recommendations in BRE Digest 498[22].

DISPLAY LIGHTING IN ALL TYPES OF SPACE

64 Reasonable provision for display lighting would be to demonstrate that the installed display lighting has an average initial (100 hour) efficacy of not less than 15 lamp-lumens per circuit-Watt. In calculating this efficacy, the power consumed by any transformers or ballasts should be taken into account.

65 Spaces where display lighting is present would normally be expected to also have general lighting for circulation and for purposes of cleaning and restocking outside public access hours. Paragraphs 55 to 63 apply to this general lighting, depending on the type of building.

CONTROLS FOR DISPLAY LIGHTING IN ALL TYPES OF SPACE

66 A way of meeting the requirement would be to connect display lighting in dedicated circuits that can be switched off at times when people will not be inspecting exhibits or merchandise or being entertained. In a retail store, for example, this could include timers that switch the display lighting off outside store opening hours, except for displays designed to be viewed from outside the building through **display windows.**

ENERGY METERS

67 The aim for buildings as a whole is to enable building occupiers to assign at least 90% of the estimated annual energy consumption of each fuel to the various end-use categories (heating, lighting etc).

68 Reasonable provision for energy meters in existing buildings would be install energy metering systems in the building service systems provided as part of the works in accordance with the recommendations in CIBSE TM 39.

69 In addition to this:

a.   Meters should be provided to enable the performance of any LZC system provided as part of the works to be separately monitored; and

b.   in buildings with a **total useful floor area** greater than 1000m^2, the metering system should enable automatic meter reading and data collection.

COMMISSIONING

70 The building services systems should be commissioned so that at completion, the system(s) and their controls are left in working order and can operate efficiently for the purposes of the conservation of fuel and power. In order to demonstrate that the heating and hot water systems have been adequately commissioned, Regulation 20C states that:

20C.–(1) This regulation applies to building work in relation to which paragraph L1(b) of Schedule 1 imposes a requirement.

(2) Where this regulation applies the person carrying out the work shall, for the purpose of ensuring compliance with paragraph L1(b) of Schedule 1, provide to the local authority a notice confirming that all fixed building services have been properly commissioned in accordance with a procedure approved by the Secretary of State.

(3) The notice shall be given to the local authority not later than the date on which the notice required by regulation 15(4), or regulation 16A(3) is given.

---

[22]   BRE Digest 498 *Selecting Lighting Controls*, BRE, 2006.

71 The procedure approved by the Secretary of State is set out in:

a. CIBSE Commissioning Code M on Commissioning Management[23]; and

This provides guidance on the overall process and includes a schedule of all the relevant guidance documents relating to the commissioning of specific building services systems.

b. The procedures for leakage testing of ductwork set out in paragraphs 73 and 74

72 The notice should include a declaration signed by a suitably qualified person confirming that:

a. a commissioning plan has been followed so that every system has been inspected and commissioned in an appropriate sequence and to a reasonable standard.

b. the results of tests confirm that the performance is reasonably in accordance with the proposed building designs, including written commentaries where excursions are proposed to be accepted.

Membership of the Commissioning Specialists Association or the Commissioning group of the HVCA may be a way of demonstrating suitability to sign the report in respect of the HVAC systems. For lighting control systems, suitability may be demonstrated by accreditation under the Lighting Industry Commissioning Scheme.

73 Ductwork leakage testing should be carried out in accordance with the procedures set out in HVCA DW/143[24] on systems served by fans with a design flow rate greater than 1m³/s and for those sections of ductwork where the pressure class is such that DW/143 recommends testing. Low pressure ductwork should be tested using the DW/143 testing provisions for medium pressure ductwork.

Membership of the HVCA specialist ductwork group or the Association of Ductwork Contractors and Allied Services could be a way of demonstrating suitable qualifications for this testing work.

74 If a ductwork system fails to meet the leakage standard, remedial work should be carried out as necessary to achieve satisfactory performance in re-tests and further ductwork sections should be tested as set out in DW/143.

Controlled fittings

75 Where windows, roof windows, rooflights or doors are to be provided, reasonable provision would be draught-proofed units whose area-weighted average performance is no worse than that given in Table 5. Column (a) applies to fittings provided as part of constructing an extension. Column (b) applies to replacement fittings or new fittings installed in an existing building.

Table 5 **Standards for controlled fittings (W/m²·K)**

Fitting	(a) Standard for new fittings in extensions	(b) Standard for replacement fittings in an existing building
Windows, roof windows and glazed rooflights[1,4]	1.8 for the whole unit OR 1.2 centre pane	2.2 for the whole unit OR 1.2 centre pane
Alternative option for windows in buildings that are essentially domestic in character[2], a window energy rating[3] of	Band D	Band E
Pedestrian doors where the door has more than 50% of its internal face area glazed	2.2	2.2
High usage entrance doors for people	6.0	6.0
Vehicle access and similar large doors	1.5	1.5
Roof ventilators (including smoke extract ventilators)	6.0	6.0

Notes:

1. **Display windows** are not required to meet the standard given in this table.

2. For example, student accommodation, care homes and similar uses where the occupancy levels and internal gains are essentially domestic in character.

3. As defined in 'Windows for new and existing housing', CE66, EST. Controlled fittings.

4. See paragraph 14.

---

[23] CIBSE Commissioning Code M: *Commissioning management*, CIBSE, 2003.

[24] DW/143 *A Practical Guide to Ductwork Leakage Testing*, HVCA, 2000.

[25] CE66 *Windows for new and existing housing*, EST.

76 The U-value or Window Energy Rating for windows can be taken as that for:

a. the standard configuration referred to in BR 443; or

b. for the specific size and configuration of the actual window.

SAP 2005[26] Table 6e gives values for different window configurations that can be used in the absence of test data or calculated values

77 In certain classes of building with high internal gains, a less demanding U-value for glazing may be an appropriate way of reducing overall CO_2 emissions. If this case can be made, then the average U-value for windows, doors and rooflights can be relaxed from the values given in Table 4, but the value should not exceed 2.7W/m²·K.

78 The overall U-value of curtain walling should be no greater than 0.9 + 1.3X, where X is the fraction of the curtain wall that is glazed.

---

[26] The Government's Standard Assessment Procedure for the energy rating of dwellings, SAP 2005, Defra.

Section 3: Guidance on thermal elements

THE PROVISION OF THERMAL ELEMENTS

This means that if the area of curtain walling is to be 60% glazed and 40% opaque, the U-value standard should be 0.9 + 1.3 x 0.6 = 1.7W/m²·K.

79 New thermal elements must comply with requirement L1(a)(i). Work on existing thermal elements is covered by regulation 4A which states:

4A.–(1) Where a person intends to renovate a thermal element, such work shall be carried out as is necessary to ensure that the whole thermal element complies with the requirements of paragraph L1(a)(i) of Schedule 1. EP s2A(2)(c)

(2) Where a thermal element is replaced, the new thermal element shall comply with the requirements of paragraph L1(a)(i) of Schedule 1.

80 Where *thermal elements* are newly constructed or replaced, reasonable provision to limit heat gains and losses through the elements must be made.

81 Reasonable provision for newly constructed *thermal elements* such as those constructed as part of an extension would be to meet the standards set out in column (a) of Table 6. In addition, no individual element should have a U-value worse than those set out in column (b) of Table 3.

82 Reasonable provision for those *thermal elements* constructed as replacements for existing elements would be to meet the standards set out in column (b) of Table 6. In addition, no individual element should have a U-value worse than those set out in column (b) of Table 3.

Curtain walling is treated as a controlled fitting and guidance is given in paragraph 78.

Continuity of insulation

83 The building fabric should be constructed so that there are no reasonably avoidable thermal bridges in the insulation layers caused by gaps within the various elements, at the joints between elements and at the edges of elements such as those around window and door openings. Reasonable provision should also be made to reduce unwanted air leakage through the new envelope parts.

84 A suitable approach to showing the requirement has been achieved would be to submit a report signed by a suitably qualified person confirming that appropriate design details and building techniques have been specified, and that the work has been carried out in ways that can be expected to achieve reasonable conformity with the specifications. Reasonable provision would be:

a. For domestic style construction, to adopt design details such as those set out in the TSO Robust Details catalogue[27]; or

Table 6 **Standards for *thermal elements* (W/m²·K)**

Element[1]	Standard for new thermal elements	Standard for replacement thermal elements
Wall	0.30	0.35[2]
Pitched roof – insulation at ceiling level	0.16	0.16
Pitched roof – insulation at rafter level	0.20	0.20
Flat roof or roof with integral insulation	0.20	0.25
Floors[3]	0.22[4]	0.25[4]

Notes:

1 'Roof' includes the roof parts of dormer windows and 'wall' includes the wall parts of dormer windows.

2 A lesser provision may be appropriate where meeting such a standard would result in a reduction of more than 5% in the internal floor area of the room bounded by the wall.

3 The U-value of the floor of an extension can be calculated using the exposed perimeter and floor area of the whole enlarged building.

4 A lesser provision may be appropriate where meeting such a standard would create significant problems in relation to adjoining floor levels.

27 *Limiting thermal bridging and air leakage: Robust construction details for dwellings and similar buildings,* Amendment 1, TSO, 2002. See www.est.org.uk

A list of additional approved details may be provided in due course.

b. For cladding systems, to adopt the guidance given in the MCRMA Technical Note[28].

c. An alternative would be to demonstrate, using the guidance in BRE IP 1/06[29], that the proposed details deliver an appropriate level of performance.

RENOVATION OF THERMAL ELEMENTS

85 Where a *thermal element* is being renovated reasonable provision in most cases would be to achieve the standard set out in column (b) of Table 7. Where the works apply to less than 25% of the surface area however reasonable provision could be to do nothing to improve energy performance.

86 If such an upgrade is not technically or functionally feasible or would not achieve a simple payback of 15 years or less, the element should be upgraded to the best standard that is technically and functionally feasible and which can be achieved within a simple payback of no greater than 15 years. Guidance on this approach is given in Appendix A in ADL1B.

RETAINED THERMAL ELEMENTS

87 Part L applies to *thermal elements* in the following circumstances:

a. where an existing thermal element is part of a building subject to a material change of use;

b. where an existing element is to become part of the thermal envelope and is to be upgraded;

c. where an existing element is being upgraded as a consequential improvement (regulation 17D) in accordance with paragraphs 14 to 23.

88 Reasonable provision would be to upgrade those *thermal elements* whose U-value is worse than the threshold value in column (a) of Table 7 to achieve the U-value given in column (b) of Table 7, provided this is technically, functionally and economically feasible. A reasonable test of economic feasibility is to achieve a *simple payback* of 15 years or less. Where the standard given in column (b) is not technically, functionally or economically feasible, then the element should be upgraded to the best standard that is technically and functionally feasible and which meets a simple payback criterion of 15 years.

Examples of where lesser provision than column (b) might apply are where the thickness of the additional insulation might reduce usable floor area by more than 5% or create difficulties with adjoining floor levels, or where the weight of the additional insulation might not be supported by the existing structural frame.

Table 7 **Upgrading retained thermal elements**

Element[1]	(a) Threshold U-value W/m²·K	(b) Improved U-value W/m²·K
Cavity Wall	0.70	0.35[2]
Other Wall type	0.70	0.35[3]
Pitched roof – insulation at ceiling level	0.35	0.16
Pitched roof – insulation at rafter level	0.35	0.20
Flat roof or roof with integral insulation	0.35	0.25
Floors[4]	0.35	0.25[5]

Notes:

1   'Roof' includes the roof parts of dormer windows and 'wall' includes the wall parts (cheeks) of dormer windows.

2   This only applies in the case of a cavity wall capable of accepting insulation. Where this is not the case it should be treated as for 'other wall type'.

3   A lesser provision may be appropriate where meeting such a standard would result in a reduction of more than 5% in the internal floor area of the room bounded by the wall.

4   The U-value of the floor of an extension can be calculated using the exposed perimeter and floor area of the whole enlarged building.

5   A lesser provision may be appropriate where meeting such a standard would create significant problems in relation to adjoining floor levels.

28   Technical Note 14: *Guidance for the design of metal cladding and roofing to comply with Approved Document L2*, MCRMA. www.mcra.co.uk.

29   IP 1/06 *Assessing the effects of thermal bridging at junctions and around openings in the external elements of buildings*, BRE, 2006.

Section 4: Providing information

89 In accordance with Requirement L1(c), the owner of the building should be provided with sufficient information about the building, the **fixed building** services and their maintenance requirements so that the building can be operated in such a manner as to use no more fuel and power than is reasonable in the circumstances.

Building log-book

90 A way of showing compliance would be to produce the necessary information following the guidance in CIBSE TM 31 Building Log Book Toolkit[30], or to add it to the existing Log Book where this already exists. If an alternative guidance document is followed in preparing the Log Book, then the information conveyed and the format of presentation should be equivalent to TM 31.

91 The information should be presented in templates as or similar to those in the TM. The information should be provided in summary form, suitable for day-to-day use. It could draw on or refer to information available as part of other documentation, such as the Operation and Maintenance Manuals and the Health and Safety file required by the CDM Regulations[31].

92 The new or updated Log Book should provide details of:

a. Any newly provided, renovated or upgraded **thermal elements** or controlled fittings;

b. any newly provided **fixed building services**, their method of operation and maintenance;

c. any newly installed energy meters; and

d. any other details that collectively enable the energy consumption of the building and building services comprising the works to be monitored and controlled.

[30] TM 31 *Building Log Book Toolkit*, CIBSE, 2006.

[31] The Construction (Design and Management) Regulations 1994, Statutory Instrument SI 1994/3140.

Section 5: Definitions

93 *BCB* means Building Control Body: a local authority or an approved inspector.

94 *Consequential improvement* means those energy efficiency improvements required by regulation 17D.

95 *A conservatory* is an extension to a building which:

a. has not less than three quarters of its roof area and not less than one half of its external wall area made from translucent material and.

b. is thermally separated from the building by walls, windows and doors with the same U-value and draught-stripping provisions as provided elsewhere in the building.

96 *Daylit space* means any space:

a. within 6m of a window wall, provided that the glazing area is at least 20% of the internal area of the window wall.

b. below rooflights and similar provided that the glazing area is at least 10% of the floor area. The normal light transmittance of the glazing should be at least 70%, or, if the light transmittance is reduced below 70%, the glazing area could be increased proportionately.

97 *Display window* means an area of glazing, including glazed doors, intended for the display of products or services on sale within the building, positioned at the external perimeter of the building, at an access level and immediately adjacent to a pedestrian thoroughfare. There should be no permanent workspace within one glazing height of the perimeter. Glazing that extends beyond 3m above such an access level is not part of a ***display window*** except:

a. where the products on display require a greater height of glazing;

b. in existing buildings, when replacing ***display windows*** that already extend to a greater height.

c. in cases of building work involving changes to the façade and glazing and requiring planning consent, where planners have discretion to require a greater height of glazing, e.g. to fit in with surrounding buildings or to match the character of the existing façade.

It is expected that ***display windows*** will be found in buildings in use classes A1, A2, A3 and D2 as detailed in Table 8.

Table 8 **Building classes**

Class	Use
A1	Shops including retail-warehouse, undertakers, showrooms, post offices, hairdressers, shops for sale of cold food for consumption off premises
A2	Financial and professional services banks, building societies, estate and employment agencies, betting offices
A3	Food and drink restaurants, pubs, wine bars, shops for sale of hot food for consumption off premises
D2	Assembly and leisure cinemas, concert halls, bingo halls, casinos, sports and leisure uses

98 *Dwelling* means a self-contained unit designed to be used separately to accommodate a single household.

99 *Emergency escape lighting* means that part of emergency lighting that provides illumination for the safety of people leaving an area or attempting to terminate a dangerous process before leaving an area.

100 *Energy efficiency requirements* means the requirements of Regulations 4A, 17C and 17D and Part L of Schedule 1.

101 *Fitout work* means that work needed to complete the internal layout and servicing of the building shell to meet the specific needs of an incoming occupier. The building shell is the structural and non-structural envelope of a building provided as a primary stage (usually for a speculative developer) for a subsequent project to fit out with internal accommodation works.

102 *Fixed building services* means any part of, or any controls associated with:

a. fixed internal or external lighting systems but does not include emergency escape lighting and specialist process lighting; or

b. (b) fixed systems for heating, hot water service systems, air conditioning or mechanical ventilation

103 *High usage entrance door* means a door to an entrance that is expected to experience large traffic volumes, and where robustness and/or powered operation is the primary performance requirement. To qualify as a ***high usage entrance door,*** the door should be equipped with automatic closers, and except where operational requirements preclude, be protected by a lobby.

104 Principal works means the work necessary to achieve the client's purposes in extending the building and/or increasing the installed capacity of any ***fixed building services***. The value of the ***principal works*** is the basis for determining a reasonable provision of ***Consequential improvements.***

105 *Renovation in* relation to a thermal element means the provision of a new layer in the thermal element or the replacement of an existing layer, but excludes decorative finishes, and 'renovate' shall be construed accordingly.

Examples of decorative finishes are paint and wall paper etc that add no appreciable thermal resistance. Dry-lining and external renders are not decorative finishes because they add thermal resistance.

106 *Room for residential purposes* means a room, or a suite of rooms, which is not a dwelling-house or a flat and which is used by one or more persons to live and sleep and includes a room in a hostel, a hotel, a boarding house, a hall of residence or a residential home, whether or not the room is separated from or arranged in a cluster group with other rooms, but does not include a room in a hospital, or other similar establishment, used for patient accommodation and, for the purposes of this definition, a 'cluster' is a group of rooms for residential purposes which is:

a. separated from the rest of the building in which it is situated by a door which is designed to be locked; and

b. not designed to be occupied by a single household.

107 *Simple payback* means the amount of time it will take to recover the initial investment through energy savings, and is calculated by dividing the marginal additional cost of implementing an energy efficiency measure by the value of the annual energy savings achieved by that measure taking no account of VAT.

a. The marginal **additional** cost is the additional cost (materials and labour) of incorporating (e.g.) additional insulation, not the whole cost of the work.

b. the cost of implementing the measure should be based on prices current at the date the proposals are made known to the **BCB** and be confirmed in a report signed by a suitably qualified person.

c. the annual energy savings should be estimated using an energy calculation tool approved by the Secretary of State pursuant to Regulation 17A; and

d. for the purposes of this Approved Document, the following energy prices should be used when evaluating the value of the annual energy savings:

   i. Mains gas – 1.45 p/kWh

   ii. Electricity – 5.0 p/kWh

   iii. Heating oil – 1.90 p/kWh

   iv. LPG – 3.39 p/kWh

For example if the additional cost of implementing a measure was £4300 and the value of the annual energy savings was £384/year, the simple payback would be (4300/384) = 11.2 years.

Energy prices are increasing significantly so building owners may wish to use higher values such as those prevailing when they apply for Building Regulations approval.

108 *Specialist process lighting* means lighting intended to illuminate specialist tasks within a space rather than the space itself. It could include theatre spotlights, projection equipment, lighting in TV and photographic studios, medical lighting in operating theatres and doctors' and dentists' surgeries, illuminated signs, coloured or stroboscopic lighting, and art objects with integral lighting such as sculptures, decorative fountains and chandeliers.

109 *Thermal element* is defined in Regulation 2A as follows.

(2A) In these Regulations 'thermal element' means a wall, floor or roof (but does not include windows, doors, roof windows or roof-lights) which separates a thermally conditioned part of the building ('the conditioned space') from:

a. the external environment (including the ground); or

b. in the case of floors and walls, another part of the building which is:

   i.   unconditioned;

   ii.   an extension falling within class VII of Schedule 2; or

   iii.   where this paragraph applies, conditioned to a different temperature,

and includes all parts of the element between the surface bounding the conditioned space and the external environment or other part of the building as the case may be.

(2B) Paragraph (2A)(b)(iii) only applies to a building which is not a dwelling, where the other part of the building is used for a purpose which is not similar or identical to the purpose for which the conditioned space is used.

110 *Total useful floor area is the total area* of all enclosed spaces measured to the internal face of the external walls. The area of sloping surfaces such as staircases, galleries, raked auditoria, and tiered terraces should be taken as their area on plan. It includes the areas occupied for example by partitions, columns, chimney breasts and internal structural or party walls. It excludes areas that are not enclosed such as open floors, covered ways and balconies.

This equates to the gross floor area as measured in accordance with the guidance issued to surveyors by the RICS.

---

32   Simplified Building Energy Model (SBEM) user manual and Calculation Tool, available at www.odpm.gov.uk

Documents referred to

BRE
www.bre.co.uk

BR 262 *Thermal insulation: avoiding risks*, 2001.
ISBN 1 86081 515 4

BR 364 *Solar Shading of Buildings*, 1999.

BR 443 *Conventions for U-value calculations*, 2006.
(Downloadable from www.bre.co.uk/uvalues.)

BRE Digest 498 *Selecting Lighting Controls*, 2006.
ISBN 1 86081 905 2

Information Paper IP1/06 *Assessing the effects of thermal bridging at junctions and around openings in the external elements of buildings*, 2006.
ISBN 1 86081 904 4

Simplified Building Energy Model (SBEM) user manual and Calculation Tool.
(Available at www.odpm.gov.uk.)

Centre for Window and Cladding Technology
www.cwct.co.uk

Thermal assessment of window assemblies, curtain walling and non-traditional building envelopes, CWCT 2006. ISBN 1 87400 338 6

CIBSE
www.cibse.org

CIBSE Commissioning Code M: *Commissioning Management*, 2003. ISBN 1 90328 733 2

TM 31 *Building Log Book Toolkit*, CIBSE, 2006.
ISBN 1 90328 771 5

TM 37 *Design for improved solar shading control*, 2006. ISBN 1 90328 757 X

TM 39 *Building energy metering*, 2006.
ISBN 1 90328 707 7

Department of the Environment, Food and Rural Affairs (Defra)
www.defra.gov.uk

The Government's Standard Assessment Procedure for energy rating of dwellings, SAP, 2005.
(Download from www.bre.co.uk/sap2005.)

Department of Transport, Local Government and the Regions (DTLR)

Limiting thermal bridging and air leakage: Robust construction details for dwellings and similar buildings, Amendment 1. Published by TSO, 2002.
ISBN 0 11753 631 8
(Download from Energy Saving Trust (EST) website on http://portal.est.org.uk/housingbuildings/calculators/robustdetails/.)

Energy Saving Trust (EST)
www.est.org.uk

CE66 *Windows for new and existing housing.*

English Heritage
www.english-heritage.org.uk

Building Regulations and Historic Buildings, 2002 (revised 2004).

Health and Safety Executive (HSE)
www.hse.gov.uk

L24 *Workplace Health, Safety and Welfare: Workplace (Health, Safety and Welfare) Regulations 1992, Approved Code of Practice and Guidance, The Health and Safety Commission*, 1992.
ISBN 0 71760 413 6

Heating and Ventilating Contractors Association

DW/143 *A practical guide to ductwork leakage testing*, HVCA 2000. ISBN 0 90378 330 4

DW/144 *Specification for sheet metal ductwork*, HVCA 1998. ISBN 0 90378 327 4

Metal Cladding and Roofing Manufacturers Association
www.mcrma.co.uk

Guidance for design of metal cladding and roofing to comply with Approved Document L2.

National Association of Rooflight Manufacturers
www.narm.org.uk

Use of rooflights to satisfy the 2002 Building Regulations for the Conservation of Fuel and Power.

NBS (on behalf of ODPM)
www.thebuildingregs.com

Low or Zero Carbon Energy Sources: Strategic guide, 2006. ISBN 1 85946 224 3

Non-domestic Heating, Cooling and Ventilation Compliance Guide, 2006. ISBN 1 85946 226 X

Thermal Insulation Manufacturers and Suppliers Association (TIMSA)
www.timsa.org.uk

HVAC Guidance for Achieving Compliance with Part L of the Building Regulations, 2006.

Legislation

SI 1991/1620 Construction Products Regulations 1991.

SI 1992/2372 Electromagnetic Compatibility Regulations 1992.

SI 1994/3051 Construction Products (Amendment) Regulations 1994.

SI 1994/3080 Electromagnetic Compatibility (Amendment) Regulations 1994.

SI 1994/3140 The Construction (Design and Management) Regulations 1994.

SI 1994/3260 Electrical Equipment (Safety) Regulations 1994.

SI 2001/3335 Building (Amendment) Regulations 2001.

SI 2006/652 Building and Approved Inspectors (Amendment) Regulations 2006.